# LOW CALORIE COOK BOOK

# LOW CALORIE COOK BOOK

*By :*

**Sneha R. Vij**

**Crest Publishing House**
(A JAICO ENTERPRISE)
G-2, 16 Ansari Road, Darya Ganj
New Delhi-110 002

LOW CALORIE COOK BOOK
ISBN 81-242-0192-7

First Edition : 2000

*Published by:*
CREST PUBLISHING HOUSE
(A Jaico Enterprise)
G-2, 16 Ansari Road, Darya Ganj,
New Delhi-110 002

*Printed by:*
Efficient Offset Printers
215, Shahzada Bagh Industrial Complex
Phase II, Delhi-110 035

# INTRODUCTION

*(A VALUABLE COLLECTION OF APPETISING CALORIE COUNTED RECIPES)*

*LOSE WEIGHT WHILE EATING WELL. MAKE COMPLETE MENUS FROM THESE DELICIOUS, CALORIE-COUNTED RECIPES FOR STARTERS, MAIN COURSES, DESSERTS & DRINKS.*

This book is a valuable collection of imaginative calorie-counted recipes to help you lose weight by following a sensible balanced diet.

Treat this book as if it were a menu & pick out combinations of dishes that appeal to you & at the same time total the requisite daily number of calories.

Keeping in mind that most of the slimmers still need to cook meals for other people & naturally do not want to prepare different food for them, the receipes in this book have been carefully planned, so that you can enjoy the same food as your family & friends.

You can use skimmed milk instead of dairy milk which is much low in calories. Low-fat yoghurt prepared with skimmed milk is not only low in calories but exceptionally nutritious too. It is also much thicker.

By using non-stick pans, you can easily reduce the amount of fat you consume or use the grill instead of the frying pan.

It is very important to be realistic about the time it may take you to reach your target weight. It is much better to do this gradually by keeping within your daily calorie allowance rather than skipping meals. In this way you will not only lose weight but will gain vitality as well.

With so many recipes to choose from, dieting need never be dull.

# CONTENTS

## PART I



## PART II

## RECIPE SECTION

# PART I

## (A) GLOSSARY OF COOKERY TERMS

| | | |
|---|---|---|
| BAKE | : | To cook by dry heat in an oven. |
| BASTE | : | To dot with fat or butter. |
| BATTER | : | Ingredients beaten alongwith some liquid to a paste. |
| BEAT | : | To introduce air into a mixture using a wooden spoon, fork, wire whisk or beater. |
| BIND | : | To add a liquid, melted fat or egg to a dry mixture in order to hold it together. |
| BLIND | : | To mix well together. |
| BLANCH | : | To skin after putting in boiling water. |
| BOIL | : | To cook at boiling point. |
| BROIL | : | Roast without fat. |
| BRUSH | : | To apply fat, milk etc lightly. |
| CHOP | : | To cut into very small pieces with a sharp knife. |
| CHILL | : | To cool over ice or in the refrigerator. |
| COAT | : | To cover food with a thin layer of egg, flour, breadcrumbs etc. |

| | | |
|---|---|---|
| COLANDER | : | A vessel having tiny holes in the bottom, used as a strainer. |
| CONSISTENCY | : | A term describing the texture, usually the thickness of a mixture. |
| COMBINE | : | To mix. |
| CUBES | : | Small equal pieces, usually of about half inch each. |
| DEEP FRY | : | To cook food in a deep layer of hot fat. |
| DICE | : | To cut into small cubes. |
| DISSOLVE | : | To make a solution with a liquid & a dry substance e.g. milk & water. |
| DOT | : | To cover the surface of a food with small amounts of fat, chocolate, nuts etc. |
| DOUGH | : | A mixture of flour & liquid thick enough to be kneaded & rolled. |
| DRAIN | : | To remove extra fat or liquid. |
| FAT | : | Ghee, oil, or butter. |
| FOLD IN | : | To combine two mixtures using a spoon or wire whisk until thoroughly mixed. |
| FRY | : | To cook in fat. |
| GARNISH | : | To decorate. |
| GRATE | : | To reduce to small pieces by rubbing through a grater. |

| | | |
|---|---|---|
| KNEAD | : | To work dough in order to make it smooth. |
| MARINATE | : | To soak food in liquid that will flavour it. |
| MELT | : | To heat solid ingredients until they become liquid. |
| MIX | : | To stir usually with a spoon until the ingredients are thoroughly combined. |
| MASH | : | To crush to pulp. |
| MINCE | : | To cut into very fine pieces. |
| PARE | : | Peel the outer skin. |
| PUREE | : | A smooth thick mixture obtained by passing cooked food through a sieve. |
| PRE-HEAT | : | To heat oven to a stated temperature before product goes in it. |
| PARBOIL | : | To half boil. |
| POACH | : | To cook eggs without shells in boiling water. |
| REHEAT | : | To heat again. |
| SAUTE | : | To fry foods in a small quantity of fat till tender. |
| SIFT | : | To pass through a fine sieve. |
| SOAK | : | To soak in liquid for a specified period of time. |
| STEW | : | To cook slowly in a small amount of liquid for a long time. |
| STIR | : | To mix with a rotary motion. |

STOCK : The liquid in which meat, vegetables etc are cooked.

SCALD : To cook or heat a liquid short of boiling.

SEASON : To add spices

SHALLOW FRY : To fry with a small quantity of fat.

SHRED : To cut into long, narrow, strips.

SIMMER : To cook gently over a low flame below the boiling point.

SPRING : Bunch.

STEAM COOL : To cook with steam as in a pressure cooker

TOSS : To lightly mix ingredients without mashing them.

UNTIL SET : Until the liquid becomes firm, as in the case of ice-creams

WHIP : To beat rapidly to produce expansion as in egg-whites.

## (A) ABBREVIATIONS USED IN THIS BOOK

| | | |
|---|---|---|
| tsp | — | teaspoon/s |
| dtsp | — | dessertspoon/s |
| tbsp | — | tablespoon/s |
| ml | — | millilitre/s |
| lit | — | litre/s |
| gm | — | gram/s |
| kg | — | kilogram/s |
| $^0$C | — | degrees centigrade |
| $^0$F | — | degrees fahrenheit |
| fridge | — | refrigerator |
| & | — | and |
| " | — | inch (e.g 1" = 1 inch) |
| mt | — | minute/s |
| hr | — | hour./s |
| ing | — | ingredient/s |
| to taste | — | as per requirement |

# *PART II* : RECIPE SECTION

## A. SOUPS

Soup is not only an excellent starter but it can also make a satisfying meal for slimmers and the calorie conscious. Choose from the wide variety of soups presented here, from the sophisticated to the substantial. Refreshing iced soups are ideal for light summer meals, served with a tangy salad; they also provide an elegant first course for a party or special occasion.

# 1. DELICIOUS CARROT SOUP

## Serve—4

*Calories—91 per portion*

*Ingredients*

| | | |
|---|---|---|
| Carrots (peeled & chopped) | — | 450 gms |
| Onion (chopped finely) | — | 1 |
| Ginger (ground to a paste) | — | ¼" |
| Orange rind (grated) | — | 1 tsp |
| Skimmed milk | — | 300 ml |
| Coriander leaves | — | 1 tsp |
| Olive oil | — | 1 tbsp |
| Chicken stock | — | 600 ml |
| Carrot slivers | — | to garnish |
| Coriander leaves | — | to garnish |
| Chilli powder | — | to taste |
| Pepper | — | to taste |
| Salt | — | to taste |

## *Method :*

1. Heat the oil in a pan & fry the onion lightly.
2. Then add the carrots & fry for 2-3 mts more.
3. Add all other ings mentioned above & bring to a boil,covered.
4. Uncover & let simmer on a low flame for 20-25 mts until the carrots are tender.
5. Blend the soup until smooth in a liquidiser.
6. Reheat & serve garnished with carrot slivers & coriander leaves.

***USEFUL TIP :*** *Cooking the carrots in olive oil makes the soup taste better than using any other fat or oil.*

# 2. TOMATO—CARROT WONDER

## Serves—4

*Calories—38 per portion*

*Ingredients :*

| | |
|---|---|
| Tomatoes (chopped) | — 400 gms |
| Carrots (grated) | — 2 |
| Onion (chopped finely) | — 1 |
| Vegetable stock | — 300 ml |
| Oregano | — 1 tsp |
| Nutmeg (grated) | — 1/8 tsp |
| Bay leaf | — 1 |
| Brown sugar | — 1 tsp |
| Parsley (chopped) | — to garnish |

## *Method :*

1. Bring the tomatoes to a boil along with rest of the ings in a heavy-bottomed pan.
2. Remove the bay leaf & serve hot garnished with parsley.

# 3. RICH ALMOND SOUP

## Serves—4

*Calories—156 per portion*

*Ingredients :*

| | |
|---|---|
| Celery sticks (chopped finely) | — 6 |
| Almonds (blanched & chopped) | — 50 gms |
| Onion (chopped finely) | — 1 |
| Parsley (chopped) | — 1 tbsp |
| Egg yolk | — 1 |
| Low-fat yoghurt | — 3 tbsps |
| Skimmed milk | — 300 ml |
| Chicken stock | — 300 ml |
| Dill seeds | — 1 tsp |
| Almonds (toasted) | — to garnish) |

## *Method :*

1. Bring to a boil the milk, stock, almonds, onion, parsley, celery, dill seeds in a heavy—bottomed pan.
2. Let simmer for 10-15 mts until the vegetables are soft.
3. Blend the soup in a liquidiser until smooth.
4. Beat the egg yolk with yoghurt & stir into the soup.
5. Reheat till warm but do not allow the soup to boil.
6. Garnish with toasted almonds & serve.

# 4. DELICIOUS RICE SOUP

## Serves—4

*Calories—94 per portion*

*Ingredients :*

|  | |  |
|---|---|---|
| Rice (long-grain) | — | 50 gms |
| Eggs | — | 2 |
| Chicken stock | — | 1½ litres |
| Lemon rind (grated) | — | 2 tsps |
| Parsley | — | 1 sprig |
| Thyme | — | 1 sprig |
| Lemon juice | — | 2 tbsp |
| Pepper | — | to taste |
| Lemon (cut into thin slices) | — | to garnish |
| Salt | — | to taste |

## *Method :*

1. Bring the stock to a boil along with the herbs & lemon rind. Add the rice & seasoning.
2. Simmer until the rice is well-cooked & tender.
3. Beat the eggs along with the lemon juice & pour the mixture into the soup, simmering very gently on a low flame & stirring continuously until the soup thickens.
4. Remove the herb sprigs & serve immediately garnished with lemon slices.

***NOTE** : Do not let the soup boil after the egg mixture has been added to it since the eggs may curdle.*

# 5. FILLING FISH SOUP

## Serves—4

*Calories—122 per portion*

*Ingredients :*

Haddock (chopped finely) — 175 gm
Cod (chopped finely) — 175 gm
Prawns (peeled) — 2 tbsp
Onions (chopped finely) — 2
Garlic (crushed) — 2 cloves
Celery (chopped finely) — 1 stick
Tomatoes (chopped finely) — 400 gm
Bay leaves (powdered) — 2-3 pinches
Thyme (dried) — pinchful
Saffron (powdered) — pinchful
Parsley (chopped) — 1 tbsp
Vegetable oil — 1 tbsp
Lemon juice — ½ tbsp
Pepper — to taste
Boiling water — 600 ml
Sugar — ½ tsp
Salt — to taste

## *Method :*

1. Heat the oil in a heavy-bottomed pan & fry the onion lightly.
2. Add the celery & fry for a minute or two.
3. Add all other ings & bring the soup to a boil.
4. Cover & simmer for about 10 mts.
5. Serve piping hot.

# 6. FISH SOUP MAZEDAAR

## Serves—4

*Calories—177 per portion*

*Ingredients :*

| | |
|---|---|
| White fish fillet (cubed) | — 225 gms |
| Leeks (cleaned & cut into strips) | — 2 |
| Onion (chopped finely) | — 1 |
| Garlic (crushed) | — 1 clove |
| Parsley (chopped) | — 2 tbsp |
| Chicken stock | — 300 ml |
| Skimmed milk | — 300 ml |
| Natural low-fat yoghurt | — 3 tbsp |
| Olive oil | — 2 tbsp |
| Pepper | — to taste |
| Salt | — to taste |
| Egg yolk | — 1 |
| Green chillies (chopped finely) | — to garnish |

## *Method :*

1. Heat the oil in a heavy-bottomed pan & fry the onion & garlic in it gently.
2. Add all other ings (except yoghurt & egg yolk) & bring to a boil. Simmer for 12-15 mts.
3. Beat the yoghurt along with egg yolk & add to the soup, stirring continuously.
4. Heat gently without boiling.
5. Serve piping hot garnished with green chillies.

# 7. YUMMY TOMATO SOUP

## Serves—4

*Calories—58 per portion*

*Ingredients :*

| | |
|---|---|
| Tomatoes (peeled & chopped) | — 450 gms |
| Onion (chopped finely) | — 1 |
| Green chillies (seeded & chopped) | — 2 |
| Basil (dried) | — 1 tsp |
| Vegetable stock | — 750 ml |
| Tomato puree | — 1 tbsp |
| Garlic (crushed) | — 1 clove |
| Natural Low-fat yoghurt | — to garnish |
| Fresh basil leaves | — to garnish |
| Vegetable oil | — 2 tbsp |

## *Method :*

1. Heat the oil in a heavy—bottomed pan & fry the onion till transparent.
2. Add all ings mentioned above & bring to a boil.
3. Cover & simmer for 15-20 mts. Cool & mash.
4. Strain & bring to a boil.
5. Check the seasoning, garnish with yoghurt & basil leaves & serve hot.

# 8. CHICKEN SOUP LAJAWAB

## Serves—4

*Calories—95 per portion*

*Ingredients :*

|  | |  |
|---|---|---|
| Chicken (cooked & chopped) | — | 175 gm |
| Onion (chopped finely) | — | 1 |
| Skimmed milk powder (mixed with 2 tbsp water) | — | 2 tbsp |
| Oil | — | 2 tsps |
| Boiling water | — | 900 ml |
| Dried sage | — | pinchful |
| Soya sauce | — | 1 tbsp |
| Cinnamon (powdered) | — | pinchful |
| Garlic (crushed) | — | 1 clove |
| Parsley (chopped finely) | — | to taste |
| Pepper | — | to taste |
| Salt | — | to taste |

## *Method :*

1. Heat the oil in a heavy — bottomed pan & fry the onion in it until transparent.
2. Then add the cooked chicken, water, sauce, cinnamon, sage, garlic & bring the soup to a boil.
3. Let simmer for 3—4 mts.
4. Then add the milk powder paste, stirring continuously.
5. Add the salt pepper.
6. Serve immediately garnished with parsley.

***NOTE :****Do not allow the soup to boil after adding the milk powder mixture or it may curdle.*

# 9. COLD PEA SOUP

## Serves—4

*Calories—118 per portion*

### *Ingredients :*

| | |
|---|---|
| Peas (shelled) | — 350 gms |
| Potatoes (chopped finely) | — 225 gms |
| Onion (chopped finely) | — 1 |
| Chicken stock | — 900 ml |
| Mint leaves | — 1 sprig |
| Lemon rind grated | — ½ tsp |
| Lemon juice | — 2 tbsps |
| Salt | — to taste |
| Pepper | — to taste |
| Fresh mint leaves (chopped) | — to garnish |

## Method :

1. Bring the peas to a boil in a heavy—bottomed pan along with the onion, potatoes, lemon rind, juice & mint leaves.
2. Add the seasoning & simmer for 15-20 mts till the peas are tender.
3. Blend in a liquidiser & keep aside to cool.
4. Chill thoroughly & serve garnished with chopped mint leaves.

# 10. GAZPACHO

## Serves—4

*Calories—33 per portion*

### *Ingredients :*

| | |
|---|---|
| Tomatoes (peeled seeded & chopped) | — 450 gms |
| Onion (minced) | — 1 |
| Green chillies (seeded & chopped) | — 2 |
| Red chillies (seeded & chopped) | — 2 |
| Garlic (chopped) | — 2 cloves |
| Chicken stock | — 450 ml |
| Lemon juice | — 1 tbsp |
| Pepper | — to taste |
| Salt | — to taste |
| Cucumber (cut into thin slices) | — to garnish |
| Red chillies (chopped finely) | — to garnish |
| Ice cubes | — to garnish |

## *Method :*

1. Blend together all ings mentioned above (except the lemon juice & seasoning) until smooth.
2. Then add the seasoning & lemon juice.
3. Chill covered.
4. Serve very chilled in bowls garnished with an ice cube each & float cucumber slices sprinkled with little chopped red chillies on top.

# (B) STARTERS

MOSTLY QUICK & EASY TO PREPARE, MANY OF THESE STARTERS CAN ALSO BE SERVED AS A LIGHT MEAL & SOME ARE SUITABLE FOR PACKED LUNCH BOXES.

# 1. GRAPEFRUIT WONDER

## Serves—4

*Calories—25 per portion*

*Ingredients :*

| | |
|---|---|
| Grapefruits (halved) | — 2 (iarge) |
| Cucumber (diced) | — 1" |
| Carrot (grated) | — 1 |
| Green chilli (seeded & chopped) | — 1 |
| Pepper | — to taste |
| Salt | — to taste |

## *Method :*

1. Loosen the grapefruit from the skin & remove, leaving the empty half grapefruit shells intact.
2. Remove the pith & discard.
3. Chop the fruit & place in bowl with the juice.
4. Add the remaining ings & mix thoroughly.
5. Cover the bowl with cling film & chill for about 2 hours.
6. Serve the mixture by piling it into the grapefruit shells.

***USEFUL TIP :*** *If the grapefruit shells tend to roll around in the dish, carefully remove a thin slice from the base of each half with a sharp knife before filling them.*

# 2. MELON DELIGHT

## Serves—4

*Calories—85 per portion*

*Ingredients :*

| | |
|---|---|
| Small round melons (halved) | — 2 |
| Fresh orange juice | — 2 tbsps |
| Raspberries or strawberries | — 75 gm |
| cucumber slices | — few |
| Mint (chopped) | — 2 tsps |
| Orange rind (grated) | — to garnish |
| Mint leaves | — to garnish |
| Pistachios (chopped) | — to garnish |

## *Method :*

1. Discard the seeds from the melon halves & scoop the flesh into a bowl.
2. Mix together this flesh along with the raspberries or strawberries, a few cucumber slices & the mint.
3. Moisten with the orange juice & spoon the mixture back into the melon shells.
4. Chill thoroughly.
5. Serve garnished with orange rind, mint leaves & pistachios.

# 3. DELICIOUS FRUIT KEBABS

## Serves—4

*Calories—173 per portion*

### *Ingredients :*

| | |
|---|---|
| Grapefruit (peeled & segmented) | — 2 |
| Oranges | — 2 |
| Prunes (soaked in water & stoned) | — 8 |
| Red wine vinegar | — 1 tbsp |
| Vegetable oil | — 4 tbsp |
| Mint leaves (chopped) | — 2 tbsp |
| Bay leaves | — 8 |
| Pepper | — to taste |
| Salt | — to taste |

## *Method :*

1. Peel & segment 1 orange. Cut the other one into half lengthways. Peel & segment one half.
2. Squeeze the juice & grate the rind from the other half. Thread the orange & grapefruit segments & the prunes into four skewers.
3. Mix together all other ings (except the bay leaves) to prepare a dressing.
4. Pour the dressing over the prepared kebabs to coat them completely.
5. Place the kebabs under a preheated moderate grill & cook for 7—8 mts until the fruit is browned turning often.
6. Thread a bay leaf at both ends of each skewer & serve hot.

# 4. VEGETABLE ROLL

## Serves—4

*Calories—256 per portion*

*Ingredients :*

| | |
|---|---|
| Tomatoes (chopped finely) | — 2 |
| Spring onions (chopped finely) | — 2 |
| Carrot (grated) | — 1 |
| Parsley (chopped finely) | — 3 tbsp |
| Celery sticks (chopped) | — 2 |
| Green chillies (chopped finely) | — 1-2 |
| Paneer (grated) | — 225 gm |
| Hazelnuts (toasted & chopped) | — 75 gm |
| Coriander leaves (chopped finely) | — 1 tbsp |
| Pepper | — to taste |
| Salt | — to taste |

*For the coating :*

| | |
|---|---|
| Hazelnuts (toasted & chopped) | — 2 tbsp |
| Breadcrumbs | — 2 tbsp |
| Parsley (chopped) | — 3 tbsp |

## *Method :*

1. Mix together all the ings (except the sliced tomatoes) & beat the mixture well.
2. Shape it into a roll about 7.5 cm/3 inches in diameter.
3. Wrap the prepared roll in a foil & chill thoroughly in the fridge.
4. Prepare the coating by mixing together all the ings.
5. Cut the chilled roll into 4 slices & roll each slice in the coating till evenly covered.
6. Serve immediately garnished with tomato slices.

# 5. DELICIOUS FRUIT COCKTAIL

## Serves—4

*Calories—95 per portion*

*Ingredients :*

|  | |  |
|---|---|---|
| Dessert apples (chopped finely) | — | 2 |
| Grapes (halved & seeded) | — | 100 gms |
| Orange juice | — | of 1 orange |
| Orange rind (grated) | — | of 1 orange |
| Natural low-fat yoghurt | — | 2 tbsp |
| Lemon juice | — | to taste |
| Celery sticks (chopped) | — | 2 |
| Cottage cheese (diced) | — | 50 gm |
| Salt | — | to taste |
| Pepper | — | to taste |
| Lettuce leaves (shredded) | — | 1-2 |

## *Method :*

1. Sprinkle lemon juice on the apple pieces.
2. Add the celery, grapes, cheese & mix well.
3. Arrange a little lettuce in the base of four dishes & pile the cheese mixture on top.
4. Mix the juice, rind & yoghurt together & pour a little of this mixture over each cocktail.
5. Chill thoroughly & serve.

# 6. PANEER DELICACY

## Serves—4

*Calories-275 per portion*

*Ingredients :*

| | |
|---|---|
| Paneer (grated coarsely) | — 175 gm |
| Cabbage (shredded) | — 250 gm |
| Celery stick (chopped) | — 1 |
| Carrots (grated) | — 2 |
| Dessert apple (grated) | — 1 |
| Raisins | — 25 gm |
| Lemon juice | — 2 tsp |
| Natural low-fat yoghurt | — 150 ml |
| Parsley (chopped) | — to garnish |
| Pepper | — to taste |
| Salt | — to taste |

## *Method :*

1. Mix together all ings (except the yoghurt) & mix well.
2. Season the yoghurt with seasoning & stir into the salad.
3. Garnish with chopped parsley & serve at once.

# 7. YUMMY STUFFED PEARS

## Serves—4

*Calories—117 per portion*

*Ingredients :*

| | |
|---|---|
| Dessert apple (grated) | — 1 |
| Pears | — 2 (big) |
| Cottage cheese | — 100 gms |
| Walnuts (chopped) | — 25 gms |
| Raisins | — 25 gms |
| Lemon juice | — few drops |
| Worcestershire sauce | — ¼ tsp |
| Pepper | — to taste |
| Salt | — to taste |
| Tomato (cut into thin slices) | — 1 |
| Lettuce leaves | — to serve |

## *Method :*

1. Cut the pears into half lengthways.
2. Remove the core, sprinkle lemon juice & keep aside.
3. Mix together all the other ings in a bowl (except the tomato slices).
4. Pile the mixture into the pear halves, place each one on a lettuce leaf & serve at once garnished with tomato slices on lettuce leaves.

# 8. TASTY AVOCADO

## Serves—2

*Calories—299 per portion*

*Ingredients :*

| | |
|---|---|
| Avocado (halved & stoned) | — 1 (small) |
| Apple (chopped) | — 1 |
| Sultanas | — 25 gms |
| Garam masala powder | — ¼ tsp |
| Lemon juice | — 2 tbsps |
| Low-fat yoghurt | — 2 tbsps |
| Pepper | — to taste |
| Salt | — to taste |

## *Method :*

1. Remove the flesh from the avocado halves (leaving the shells intact) & cut it into small pieces.
2. Sprinkle with 1½ tbsp lemon juice.
3. Soak the sultanas into the remaining lemon juice for about 5-7 mts.
4. Mix together the apple, avocado & the sultanas.
5. Mix together the yoghurt & garam masala powder.
6. Combine the yoghurt mixture along with the apple mixture.
7. Sprinkle the seasoning & pile into the avocado shells. Serve at once.

# (C) VEGETABLES & SALAD

THE MARVELLOUS SELECTION OF VEGETABLES AVAILABLE TODAY MEANS IT IS POSSIBLE TO ENJOY EXCITING PREPARATIONS. ALL THE YEAR ROUND

# 1. SPINACH WITH YOGHURT

## Serves—4

*Calories—100 per portion*

***Ingredients :***

| | |
|---|---|
| Fresh spinach (rinsed thoroughly) | — 1 kg |
| Low-fat yoghurt | — 150 ml |
| Garlic (crushed) | — 1-2 cloves |
| Pepper | — to taste |
| Salt | — to taste |

## *Method :*

1. Cook the spinach without water in a covered pan, until tender. Drain & cool.
2. Mix together the yoghurt & garlic & stir into the spinach.
3. Sprinkle seasoning & serve at once.

***USEFUL TIP :*** *Reserve the drained liquid after boiling the spinach to give flavour to a soup of leftover vegetables.*

# 2. YUMMY VEGETABLE CURRY

## Serves—4

*Calories—180 per portion*

*Ingredients :*

|  | |  |
|---|---|---|
| French beans (chopped) | — | 225 gms |
| Cauliflower (cut into florets) | — | 1 |
| Carrots (chopped) | — | 225 gms |
| Green peas (shelled) | — | 225 gms |
| Vegetable stock | — | 450 ml |
| Coriander leaves (chopped) | — | to garnish |

***For the sauce***

|  | |  |
|---|---|---|
| Onion (chopped) | — | 1 (small) |
| Natural low-fat yoghurt | — | 150 ml |
| Ginger - garlic paste | — | 2 tsp |

|  | |  |  | |  |
|---|---|---|---|---|---|
| Flour | — | 1 tbsp | Oil | — | 1 tbsp |
| Pepper | — | to taste | Salt | — | to taste |
| Lemon juice | — | 1 tsp | Chilli powder | — | to taste |

## *Method :*

1. Simmer the vegetables in the stock for 10-12 mts until tender. Drain & reserve the stock.
2. To make the sauce, heat the oil in a heavy-bottomed pan and fry the onion lightly.
3. Add the seasoning, ginger-garlic paste & cook for another minute. Stir in the flour & cook for 1-2 mts.
4. Add the reserved stock, gradually stirring continuously.
5. Stir in the yoghurt & lemon juice. Bring to a boil & simmer for 1-2 mts.
6. Arrange the vegetables in a serving dish, pour the sauce over & serve garnished with coriander leaves.

# 3. TASTY DAL

## Serves—4

*Calories—222 per portion*

***Ingredients :***

| | |
|---|---|
| Toor dal | — 225 gms |
| Cauliflower (broken into florets) | — 175 gms |
| Onion (chopped) | — 1 |
| Button mushrooms (chopped) | — 100 gms |
| Vegetable stock | — 600 ml |
| Mustard seeds | — ½ tsp |
| Cumin seeds | — ½ tsp |
| Ginger (chopped finely) | — 1 tsp |
| Pepper | — to taste |
| Salt | — to taste |
| Chilli powder | — to taste |
| Turmeric powder | — ½ tsp |
| Corriander leaves | — to garnish |
| Lemon (cut into slices) | — to garnish |
| Onion (cut into thin rings) | — to garnish |

## *Method :*

1. Bring the dal & the stock to a boil.
2. Simmer for 35-40 mts or until the dal is tender.
3. Steam the cauliflower florets till soft.
4. Heat the oil & fry the mustard & cumin seeds for about one mt. Stir in the onion & fry for 3-4 mts more.
5. Add this seasoning to the cooked dal & simmer for 4-5 mts.
6. Before serving, sprinkle the coriander leaves, and arrange the lemon slices & onion rings on top.

# 4. MIXED VEGETABLE DELIGHT

## Serves—4

*Calories—57 per portion*

### *Ingredients :*

| | | |
|---|---|---|
| Mixed vegetables (of your choice) | — | 450 gms |
| Wine vinegar | — | 120 ml |
| Chilli powder | — | ½ tsp |
| Turmeric powder | — | ¼ tsp |
| Coriander-cumin powder | — | ½ tsp |
| Dry white wine | — | 120 ml |
| Maca (powdered) | — | 1 tsp |
| Salt | — | to taste |
| Coriander leaves (optional) | — | to garnish |

## *Method :*

1. Chop all the vegetables into medium size pieces & bring to a boil along with the wine, vinegar, spices salt & just enough water to cover the vegetables.
2. Simmer on a low flame for another 10-12 mts.
3. Serve hot garnished with coriander leaves (optional).

***NOTE :*** *The vegetables should be slightly crisp, so do not overcook.*

# 5. YUMMY CAULIFLOWER

## Serves—4

*Calories—82 per portion*

*Ingredients :*

|  | |  |
|---|---|---|
| Cauliflower (broken into florets) | — | 1 |
| Onion (chopped) | — | 1 |
| Carrots (chopped) | — | 2 |
| Ginger (ground to a paste) | — | 1 tsp |
| Coriander leaves (ground to a paste) | — | 2 tsps |
| Celery sticks (chopped) | — | 2 |
| Turmeric powder | — | ½ tsp |
| Natural low-fat yoghurt | — | 150 ml |
| Vegetable stock | — | 120 ml |
| Vegetable oil | — | 1 tbsp |
| Coriander leaves (chopped) | — | to garnish |
| Pepper | — | to taste |
| Salt | — | to taste |

## *Method :*

1. Heat the oil in a heavy-bottomed pan, add the spices & fry gently.
2. Then add the onion & fry for 1-2 mts more.
3. Stir in the remaining vegetables, the stock & sprinkle seasoning.
4. Simmer covered until the vegetables are tender.
5. This should not take more than 10-12 mts.
6. Stir in the yoghurt, garnish with the coriander leaves & serve immediately.

# 6. DELICIOUS RED CABBAGE

## Serves—4

*Calories—40 per portion*

*Ingredients :*

| | |
|---|---|
| Red cabbage (shredded) | — 1 |
| Allspice (powdered) | — ¼ tsp |
| Caraway seeds | — 2 tsps |
| Vinegar | — 1 tbsp |
| Parsley (chopped) | — to garnish |
| Salt | — to taste |

## *Method :*

1. Bring ½" depth of water to a boil in a large pan.
2. Add all the ings mentioned above, cover & cook on a medium flame until the cabbage is tender, stirring off & on.
3. Drain the cabbage & serve hot garnished with parsley.

# 7. CABBAGE DELIGHT

## Serves—4

*Calories—53 per portion*

*Ingredients :*

| | |
|---|---|
| Green cabbage (shredded) | — 350 gms |
| White cabbage (shredded) | — 350 gms |
| Poppy seeds | — 1½ tsps |
| Water | — 150 ml |
| Butter (cut into small pieces) | — 15 gms |
| Coriander leaves (garnished) | — 1 tbsp |
| Lemon rind (grated) | — ½ tsp |
| Pepper | — to taste |
| Salt | — to taste |

## *Method :*

1. Bring the water to a boil along with a little salt.
2. Add both cabbages & simmer for 8-10 mts, covered
3. If all water is not absorbed, open the lid & boil quickly
4. Add the butter, rind, pepper, poppy seeds & stir briefly until the butter is melted.
5. Serve hot garnished with coriander leaves.

# 8. ORANGE-BEAN SALAD

## Serves—4

*Calories—278 per portion*

*Ingredients :*

| | |
|---|---|
| Oranges (large) | — 4 |
| Kidney beans (boiled & drained) | — 400 gms |
| Beans prouts (boiled & drained) | — 275 gms |
| Celery sticks (thinly sliced) | — 4 |
| Coriander leaves (chopped) | — to garnish |

***For the Light French Dressing***

| | |
|---|---|
| Olive oil | — 3 tbsp |
| Lemon juice | — 2 tbsp |
| Sugar | — to taste |
| Pepper | — to taste |
| Mustard seeds (powdered) | — ¼ tsp |
| Salt | — to taste |

## *Method :*

1. To make the dressing, put all the ings into a screw-topped jar & shake well until blended.
2. Using a serrated knife, cut the top & bottom from the oranges, remove all the skin & pith, leaving a ball of fruit.
3. Cut into segments by cutting down on either side of each membrane, and put in a bowl with any juice that runs out while cutting.
4. Add the beans, beansprouts & celery & toss together lightly.
5. Just before serving the salad, spoon the dressing over.

***USEFUL TIP :*** *This crisp colourful salad is both delicious & nutritious.*

# 9. MUSHROOM SALAD

## Serves—4

*Calories—108 per portions*

*Ingredients :*

| | |
|---|---|
| Button mushrooms (stalks trimmed with caps) | — 250 mgs |
| Gherkins (chopped) | — 2 tbsps |
| Tomatoes (chopped finely) | — 175 gms |
| Lemon juice | — ½ tbsp |
| Garlic (crushed with salt) | — 2-3 clove |
| Oil | — 3 tbsps |
| Parsley (chopped finely) | — 1 sprig |
| Sugar | — to taste |
| Pepper | — to taste |

## *Method :*

1. Rinse & drain the mushrooms thoroughly.
2. Slice them thinly & sprinkle with the lemon juice. Add the other vegetables & toss to mix well.
3. To make the dressing beat together the oil, seasoning, garlic & parsley.
4. Pour this dressing over the mushroom salad & toss well to mix.
5. Chill in the fridge for about 30 mts & serve.

# 10. EGG SALAD

## Serves—4

*Calories—143 per portion*

### *Ingredients :*

| | |
|---|---|
| Lettuce leaves | — few |
| Eggs (hard-boiled & chopped finely) | — 4 |
| Cucumber (peeled & thinly sliced) | — 1 |
| Spring onions (chopped finely) | — bunchful |

### *For the sauce :*

| | |
|---|---|
| Natural low-fat yoghurt | — 300 ml |
| Mustard seeds (powdered) | — 1 tsp |
| Lemon juice | — 1 tbsp |
| Pepper | — to taste |
| Salt | — to taste |

## *Method :*

1. Arrange the lettuce leaves in a serving dish & cover with the sliced cucumber.
2. Combine the eggs & onions together & spoon into the centre.
3. To prepare the sauce, mix all the ings mentioned together.
4. Pour over the salad & serve at once.

# 11. RICE SALAD

## Serves—4

*Calories—357 per portion*

*Ingredients :*

| | |
|---|---|
| Long-grain brown rice | — 275 gms |
| Pineapple (peeled, cored & cubed) | — 1 |
| Coconut flakes | — 50 gms |
| Cucumber (peeled & cubed) | — ½ |
| Lemon juice | — 1 tsp |
| Oil | — 1 tbsp |
| Pepper | — to taste |
| Salt | — to taste |
| Almonds (blanched toasted) | — to garnish |

## *Method :*

1. Mix together all the above ings (except almonds) & toss.
2. Scatter the almonds over the salad & serve at once.

# 12. COTTAGE CHEESE SALAD

## Serves—4

*Calories—114 per portion*

*Ingredients :*

| | |
|---|---|
| Cottage cheese (crumbled) | — 100 gms |
| Cabbage (shredded finely) | — 225 gms |
| Caraway seeds (roasted & powdered) | — 1 tsp |
| Oil | — 2 tbsps |
| Lemon juice | — 2 tsps |
| Wine vinegar | — 1 tsp |
| Mustard seeds (powdered) | — ½ tsp |
| Water | — 2 tbsps |
| Green chillies (chopped finely) | — to taste |
| Pepper | — to taste |
| Salt | — to taste |

## *Method :*

1. Blend the caraway seed powder along with the oil, vinegar, lemon juice, pepper, mustard, salt, water & the cottage cheese inorder to prepare a smooth dressing.
2. Place the cabbage & chilli mixture into 4 bowls, stir well, spoon the dressing over & serve immediately.

# 13. SALAD WITH A DIFFERENCE

## Serves—4

*Calories—64 per portion*

*Ingredients :*

| | |
|---|---|
| Orange (segmented & chopped) | — 1 |
| Almonds (roasted until brown) | — 40 gms |
| Celery (chopped finely) | — 225 gms |
| Coriander seeds (powdered) | — 1 tsp |
| Low-fat yoghurt | — 150 ml |
| Cumin seeds (powdered) | — ½ tsp |
| Salt | — to taste |

## *Method :*

1. Put half the almonds along with the celery & orange in a big bowl & toss lightly.
2. Combine the yoghurt & seasoning.
3. Pour over the salad, sprinkle the remaining almonds on top & serve.

# 14. RICH CHICKEN SALAD

**Serves—4**

*Calories—254 per portion*

*Ingredients :*

| | |
|---|---|
| Chicken livers | — 450 gms |
| Walnuts (shelled & chopped) | — 25 gms |
| Garlic (crushed) | — 3-4 cloves |
| Natural low-fat yoghurt | — 3 tbsps |
| Olive oil | — 5 tsps |
| Wine vinegar | — 2 tsps |
| Lettuce (chopped finely) | — ½ |
| Radishes (thinly sliced) | — 50 gms |
| Spring onions (chopped finely) | — 4 |
| Pepper | — to taste |
| Salt | — to taste |

## *Method :*

1. Brush a heavy-bottomed pan with 1 tsp oil & heat gently.
2. Snip the chicken livers into quarters (with kitchen scissors), directly into the pan & stir on a medium flame for 3-4 mts.
3. .Add the walnut pieces, cover & simmer on a low flame for another 5 mts.
4. Blend the remaining oil with the garlic vinegar, yoghurt, seasoning in a big bowl. In another bowl, toss together the lettuce, radishes & onions.
5. Divide the vegetable mixture into 4 parts, spoon the liver quarters with the walnuts & pan juices over the vegetables & serve accompanied by the dressing.

# 15. TASTY SPINACH WITH ALMONDS

**Serves—4**

*Calories—132 per portion*

***Ingredients :***

| | |
|---|---|
| Fresh spinach (chopped) | — 1 Kg |
| Onion (chopped finely) | — ½ (big) |
| Almonds (roasted lightly and halved) | — 40 gms |
| Natural low-fat yoghurt | — 3 tbsps |
| Nutmeg (grated) | — to taste |
| Butter | — 15 gms |
| Salt | — to taste |

## *Method :*

Melt the butter in a pan and fry the onions in it till they soften. Add the spinach and coat it with the onion mixture. Season with salt and nutmeg and cook covered for 10-12 mts over a low flame. Stir in the yoghurt and remove the spinach mixture. In the same pan, fry the almonds lightly. Add the almonds to the spinach mixture and serve at once.

# 16. BROAD BEANS DELIGHT

## Serves—4

*Calories—191 per portion*

### *Ingredients :*

| | |
|---|---|
| Fresh Broad beans (boiled in salted water) | — 450 gms |
| Butter | — 15 gms |
| Sesame seeds (toasted till brown) | — 2 tbsp |
| Lemon juice | — 1 tbsp |
| Pepper | — to taste |

### *Method :*

Heat butter in a pan and add to it the drained beans. Fry till the beans brown well and add to it the pepper and lemon juice. Serve sprinkled with sesame seeds.

# (D) FISH

THIS CHAPTER SHOWS SOME IMAGINATIVE WAYS OF PREPARING THIS VERY NUTRITIOUS, HIGH-PROTEIN FOOD. CHOOSE FROM THE VAST SELECTION OF FISH & SEAFOOD THAT IS READILY AVAILABLE NOWADAYS. SOME OF THE RECIPES ARE PRIMARILY FOR ENTERTAINING WHILE OTHERS MAKE ECONOMICAL FAMILY MEALS.

# 1. STIR-FRIED FISH

## Serves—4

*Calories—192 per portion*

*Ingredients :*

| | |
|---|---|
| Cod fillet (skinned) | — 500 gm |
| Green peas (shelled & boiled) | — 50 gm |
| Sweetcorn (boiled) | — 50 gm |
| Chicken stock or water | — 6 tbsp |
| dry sherry | — 2 tsp |
| soya sauce | — 2 tsp |
| Cornflour (mixed with 1 tsp water) | — 1 tsp |
| Spring onion (sliced) | — to garnish |
| Oil | — 1 tbsp |
| Salt | — to taste |

## *Method :*

1. Cut the cod fillets into 1 inch wide strips, sprinkle with salt & keep aside for 15-20 mts.
2. Heat the oil in a pan, add the fish & stir-fry for 3-4 mts.
3. Add all other ings (except the cornflour mixture) & bring to a boil.
4. Then stir in the cornflour mixture & cook for about 1 mt.
5. Serve immediately garnished with spring onion slices.

***USEFUL TIP :*** *Stir - frying requires less fat or oil than other types of frying. It also reduces the cooking time to the minimum. The food retains colour & texture.*

# 2. FISH WITH RICE

## Serves—4

*Calories—288 per portion*

### *Ingredients :*

|  | |  |
|---|---|---|
| Haddock fillets | — | 500 gms |
| Long-grain rice | — | 150 gms |
| Egg (hard-boiled & chopped) | — | 1 |
| Skimmed milk | — | 200 ml |
| Green peas (cooked with salt) | — | 100 gms |
| Pepper | — | to taste |
| Salt | — | to taste |
| Parsley (chopped) | — | to garnish |

*Method :*

1. Poach the haddock in milk until tender.
2. Drain & reserve the liquid.
3. Cook the rice in boiling salted water until tender.
4. Drain & return to the pan.
5. Stir in the fish, peas, egg & the reserved liquid.
6. Season & let it heat on a low flame.
7. Serve hot garnished with parsley.

# 3. YUMMY FISH CASSEROLE

## Serve—4-6

*Calories—135 per portion*

*Ingredients :*

| | |
|---|---|
| Cod fillets | — 4-6 |
| Spring onions with leaves (chopped) | — 3 |
| Tomatoes (chopped) | — 400 gm |
| Green chilli (seeded & cut into strips) | — 1 |
| Red chilli (seeded & cut into strips) | — 1 |
| Lemon juice | — 1 tbsp |
| Vegetable oil | — 1 tbsp |
| Sugar | — ½ tsp |
| Salt | — to taste |
| Pepper | — to taste |
| Parsley (chopped) | — 1 tbsp |

## *Method :*

1. Heat the oil in an ovenproof casserole, add the onion & fry gently.
2. Then add the chillies & stir-fry for 2 mts more.
3. Then add the tomatoes & bring the mixture to a boil along with sugar.
4. Simmer for 2-3 mts & lay the cod on top.
5. Squeeze the lemon juice, sprinkle the seasoning, parsley & cook in the oven for 15-20 mts. Serve hot.

# 4. DELICIOUS COD WONDER

## Serves—6

*Calories—217 per portion*

***Ingredients :***

| | |
|---|---|
| Cod fillet (skinned & cubed) | — 1 kg |
| Onion (chopped) | — 1 |
| Olive oil | — 4 tbsps |
| Garlic (crushed) | — 1-2 cloves |
| Lemon juice | — 3 tbsps |
| Cinnamon | — 2" |
| Turmeric powder | — ½ tsp |
| Fish stock | — 300 ml |
| Pepper | — to taste |
| Salt | — to taste |
| Parsley (chopped) | — to garnish |

## *Method :*

1. Heat the oil & fry the onion till transparent.
2 .Add the garlic & fry for 1-2 mts more.
3. Then add the fish stock, lemon juice, turmeric & bring to a boil.
4. Then add the cinnamon & fish along with the seasoning & simmer for 10-12 mts on a low flame.
5. Serve hot garnished with parsley.

# 5. IRRESISTABLE FISH KEBABS

## Serves—4

*Calories—114 per portion*

### *Ingredients :*

| | |
|---|---|
| Cod (cut into small cubes) | — 450 gms |
| Button mushrooms (chopped) | — 8 |
| Tomatoes (quartered) | — 4 |
| Green chillies (seeded & chopped) | — 1-2 |
| Grapes (seeded) | — 12 |
| Lemon juice | — to taste |
| Coriander leaves (chopped) | — to garnish |

## *Method :*

1. Simmer the chillies in a little water for 8-10 mts. Drain.
2. Thread the fish cubes onto skewers with all other ings.
3. Sprinkle with lemon juice & coriander leaves & place under a preheated grill for 8-10 mts until the fish is well cooked, turning often serve hot.

# 6. KHATTA MEETHA MACKEREL

**Serves—4**

*Calories—400 per portion*

*Ingredients :*

| | |
|---|---|
| Mackerel (cleaned) | — 4 |
| Lemon (cut into slices) | — to garnish |

*For the marinade :*

| | |
|---|---|
| Onion (grated) | — 1 |
| Carrot (grated) | — 1 |
| Brown sugar | — 1 tbsp |
| Lemon juice | — 2 tbsps |
| Soya sauce | — 1 tbsp |
| Pepper | — to taste |
| Salt | — to taste |

## *Method:*

1. Mix together all the ings for the marinade & place the mackerel in it for 1-2 hrs.
2. Put the mackerel into an overproof dish & bake for 10-12 mts.
3. Pour the marinade over & bake for 15-20 mts more.
4. Serve hot garnished with lemon slices.

# 7. YUMMY FISH CURRY

## Serves—4

*Calories—216 per portion*

*Ingredients :*

|  |  |
|---|---|
| Haddock fillets (cubed) | — 500 gms |
| Onion (chopped) | — 1 |
| Carrot (chopped) | — 1 |
| Apple (peeled, cored & chopped) | — 1 |
| Margarine | — 25 gms |
| Green chillies (seeded & chopped) | — 1-2 |
| Garam masala powder | — 1 tsp |
| Maida | — 1 tbsp |
| Fish stock | — 300 ml |
| Lemon juice | — 1 tsp |
| Sultanas | — 1 tbsp |
| Pepper | — to taste |
| Salt | — to taste |
| Parsley (chopped) | — to garnish |

## *Method :*

1. Melt the margarine in a pan & fry the vegetables along with the garam masala powder for 3-4 mts.
2. Stir in the flour & cook for a few seconds.
3. Blend in the lemon juice & stock gradually & cook till the mixture thickens.
4. Add the rest of the ings along with the fish cubes & cook covered until the fish is tender, on a low flame.
5. Serve hot garnished with chopped parsley.

# 8. CRAB SPECIALITY

## Serves—4

*Calories—345 per portion*

*Ingredients :*

| | |
|---|---|
| Crab (cooked & cut into pieces) | — 1 (large) |
| Chicken (minced finely) | — 250 gms |
| Eggs (beaten) | — 2 |
| Black beans (chopped) | — 2 tbsps |
| Garlic (crushed) | — 2-3 cloves |
| Oil | — 2½ tbsps |
| Ginger (chopped finely) | — 2 tbsps |
| Spring onions (chopped) | — 4 |
| Chicken stock | — 300 ml |
| Dry sherry | — 2 tbsp |
| Salt | — to taste |
| Spring onion (cut into rings) | — to garnish. |

## *Method :*

1. Heat the oil in a heavy-bottomed pan, add the onions, ginger, garlic, beans & stir fry for a minute.
2. Add the chicken & brown it for a minute.
3. Then add the crab, sherry, stock & bring the mixture to a boil. Stir in the eggs.
4. Serve at once garnished with spring onion rings.

# 9. GINGER PRAWNS

## Serves—4

*Calories—320 per portion*

*Ingredients :*

| | |
|---|---|
| Prawns (boiled in salted water) | — 12 (large) |
| Spring onions (chopped) | — 8 |
| Ginger (chopped finely) | — 2" |
| Soya sauce | — 2 tbsps |
| Dry sherry | — 2 tbsps |
| Chicken stock | — 150 ml |
| Pepper | — to taste |
| Salt | — to taste |

## Method :

1. Rinse the mullets and pat dry with tissue papers. Brush with ¾ tbsp of the oil and keep aside for about 5-7 mts.
2. Heat the remaining oil in a non-stick pan and fry the corriander seeds and garlic in it for 2-3 mts.
3. Brush the fish with a little of this mixture, sprinkle with seasoning and cook under a hot grill for 4-5 mts.
4. Baste with the remaining garlic-corriander mixture, turn and grill for another 4-5 mts until crisp. Serve at once garnished with lemon slices and bay leaves.

# 10. RED MULLET DELIGHT

## Serves—4

*Calories—240 per portion*

*Ingredients :*

|  | |  |
|---|---|---|
| Red mullets (cleaned but livers not removed) | — | 4 |
| Coriander seeds (crushed) | — | ¼ tbsp |
| Olive oil | — | 2 tbsp |
| Garlic (chopped finely) | — | 2-3 cloves |
| White pepper (freshly ground) | — | to taste |
| Salt | — | to taste |
| Bay leaves | — | to garnish |
| Lemon (cut into slices) | — | to garnish |

## *Method :*

1. Bring all the ings (except the prawns) to a boil.
2. Simmer for 3-4 mts.
3. Stir in the prawns & cook covered for 2-3 mts more.
4. Serve at once.

# (E) CHICKEN

PROVIDED THAT THE FATTY SKIN IS REMOVED, CHICKEN IS DEFINITELY AN IDEAL CHOICE FOR A MAIN COURSE, BEING HIGH IN PROTEIN. MANY OF THE RECIPES IN THIS SECTION ARE SO VERY EASY TO COOK & CAN TASTE SO GOOD THAT THEY ARE REALLY GOING TO PAMPER THE TASTEBUDS OF THE EATER.

# 1. CITRUS CHICKEN

**Serves—4**

*Calories—346 per portion*

*Ingredients :*

| | |
|---|---|
| Chicken quarters (skinned) | — 4 (225 gm each) |
| Lemons or limes (large) | — 2 |
| Oranges (large) | — 2 |
| Butter | — 15 gm |
| Parsley sprigs | — to garnish |
| Cinnamon (powdered) | — to taste |
| Pepper | — to taste |
| Salt | — to taste |

## *Method :*

1. Rub the chicken quarters with salt & seasoning & place in a lightly oiled casserole.
2. Squeeze the juice from one of the lemons or limes & pour' over the chicken.
3. Grate the rind from one of the oranges.
4. Peel the remaining lemon or lime & both oranges & chop the flesh. Mix the flesh with the grated orange rind & pour over the chicken.
5. Dot the chicken & fruit with the butter, cover tightly & cook in an oven till tender.
6. Serve hot garnished with parsley.

***USEFUL TIP :*** *Limes are slightly sweeter & have a subtle flavour than lemons. You can tell a fresh lime by its dark, glossy, tight skin.*

# 2. LEMONY CHICKEN

## Serves—4

*Calories—228 per portion*

*Ingredients :*

| | | |
|---|---|---|
| Chicken portions (skinned) | — | 4 (275 gms each) |
| Onion (chopped) | — | 1 (small) |
| Celery stick (chopped) | — | 1 |
| Lemon juice | — | 1 tbsp |
| Lemon rind (grated) | — | 1 tsp |
| Chicken stock | — | 300 ml |
| Cornflour (mixed with 2 tbsps water) | — | 1 tbsp |
| Pepper | — | to taste |
| Chilli powder | — | to taste |
| Lemon (cut into slices) | — | to garnish |
| Coriander leaves (chopped) | — | to garnish |

## *Method :*

1. Cook the chicken portion covered with all ings (except cornflour) in the oven until well cooked.
2. Strain the stock & transfer the chicken to a serving dish.
3. Prepare a thick sauce by combining the cornflour paste with the strained stock by cooking on a low flame, stirring continuously.
4. Add the seasoning & pour the sauce over the chicken.
5. Serve at once garnished with coriander leaves & lemon slices.

# 3. FRUITY CHICKEN

## Serves—4

*Calories—284 per portion*

*Ingredients :*

| | |
|---|---|
| Chicken portions (skinned) | — 4 (175 gms each) |
| Banana (chopped finely) | — 1 |
| Pineapple rings (chopped finely) | — 4 |
| Chicken stock | — 250 ml |
| Chilli powder | — to taste |
| Garam masala powder | — to taste |
| Turmeric powder | — ¼ tsp |
| Salt | — to taste |
| Orange (peeled & sliced) | — to garnish |

## *Method :*

1. Put the chicken in a casserole along with the spices, cover & cook in the oven until well-cooked.
2. Add the chopped fruits & cook for further 10 mts.
3. Serve hot garnished with orange slices.

# 4. KHATTA MEETHA CHICKEN

## Serves—4

*Calories—264 per portion*

*Ingredients :*

| | |
|---|---|
| Chicken portions (skinned) | — 4 (175 gms each) |
| Onion (chopped finely) | — 1 |
| Green chillies (chopped) | — 4 |
| Red chillies (chopped) | — 2 |
| Pineapple (chopped) | — 225 gms |
| Vinegar | — 1 tbsp |
| Soya sauce | — 1 tbsp |
| Tomatoes (chopped) | — 225 gms |
| Honey | — 1 tsp |
| Water | — 150 ml |
| Salt | — to taste |

## *Method :*

1. Cook the chicken uncovered in the oven for 15-20 mts.
2. Prepare a thick sauce by bringing to a boil all other ings & then simmering for a few mts.
3. Pour this sauce over the chicken & then return to the oven & cook until tender, occasionally basting with the sauce.
4. Serve hot.

# 5. DAHI CHICKEN

## Serves—4

*Calories—491 per portion*

*Ingredients :*

| | |
|---|---|
| Chicken (cut into portions) | — 1 (1.5 kg) |
| Natural low-fat yoghurt | — 300 ml |
| Onion (chopped finely) | — 1 (large) |
| Garlic (crushed) | — 5-6 cloves |
| Green chillies (crushed) | — 4-5 |
| Chicken stock | — 600 ml |
| Ginger (crushed) | — 1" |
| Chilli powder | — to taste |
| Turmeric powder | — ½ tsp |
| Garam masala powder | — ¼ tsp |
| Cornflour (mixed with 2 tbsp water) | — 1 tbsp |
| Vegetable oil | — 2 tbsps |
| Pepper | — to taste |
| Salt | — to taste |
| Coriander leaves (chopped) | — to garnish |

## *Method :*

1. Heat the oil in a heavy-bottomed pan & stir fry the chicken pieces along with the onion, chillies, ginger, garlic, pepper, chilli powder, turmeric & garam masala powder until brown on all sides.
2. Mix together the stock & cornflour paste & cook till thickened on a low flame.
3. Pour this sauce over the chicken & simmer covered for about 20-30 mts.
4. Serve hot garnished with coriander leaves.

# 6. SPICY CHICKEN

## Serves—6

*Calories—240 per portion*

*Ingredients :*

| | |
|---|---|
| Chicken breasts (boned & skined) | — 3 |
| Onions (chopped) | — 2 (large) |
| Green chillies (seeded & chopped) | — 3-4 |
| Garlic (chopped) | — 2 cloves |
| Lemon rind (grated) | — ½ tsp |
| Cinnamon (powdered) | — 1 tsp |
| Cumin seeds | — 1 tsp |
| Paprika | — 1 tbsp |
| Red chicllies (seeded & chopped) | — 2-3 |
| Cornflour (mixed with 2 tbsps water) | — 1 tbsp |
| Natural low-fat yoghurt | — 300 ml |
| Vegetable oil | — 1 tbsp |
| Chicken stock | — 2 tbsps |
| Pepper | — to taste |
| Salt | — to taste |

## *Method :*

1. Combine the cinnamon with the yoghurt & marinate the chicken in this mixture for half-an-hour.
2. Heat the oil in an heavy-bottomed pan & fry the onions, garlic, chillies & cumin seeds lightly.
3. Then stir in the paprika.
4. Drain the chicken, reserving the liquid.
5. Add the chicken to the pan along with the stock, reserved liquid, rind & simmer covered till the chicken is tender.
6. Just before serving, stir in the cornflour paste, bring the mixture to a boil,sprinkle seasoning & serve hot with rotis or rice.

# 7. CHICKEN WITH LEEKS

## Serves—4

*Calories—189 per portion*

*Ingredients :*

| | |
|---|---|
| Boneless chicken breasts (skinned) | — 350 gms |
| Cucumber (peeled, halved & seeded) | — ½ |
| Leeks (sliced thinly) | — 3 |
| Red chillies (crushed) | — 2-3 |
| Coriander leaves (chopped) | — 1 tbsp |
| Dry sherry | — 1 tbsp |
| Soya sauce | — 1 tbsp |
| Garlic (chopped) | — 4 cloves |
| Oil | — 2 tbsps |
| Salt | — to taste |
| Coriander leaves | — to garnish |

## *Method :*

1. Cut the cucumber into small cubes, sprinkle with salt & keep aside for about half-an-hour.
2. Rinse & drain thoroughly.
3. Chop the chicken into small cubes.
4. Heat the oil in a pan & fry the leeks & garlic lightly.
5. Add the chicken cubes along with all other ings (except the cucumber) & cook till the chicken is well—cooked.
6. Lastly add the cucumber & cook for a few seconds.
7. Sprinkle the coriander leaves & serve at once.

# 8. DILBAHAR CHICKEN

## Serves—4

*Calories—208 per portion*

### *Ingredients :*

|  |  |
| --- | --- |
| Boneless chicken breasts (shredded) | — 350 gms |
| Spring onions (chopped) | — 4 |
| Sesame oil | — ½ tsp |
| White sesame seeds (roasted in little oil) | — 2 tbsps. |
| Chilli bean sauce | — ½ tsp |
| Wine vinegar | — 1 tbsp |
| Soya sauce | — 1 tbsp |
| Vegetable oil | — 2 tbsps |
| Cornflour | — 2 tsps |
| Egg white (beaten) | — 1 |
| Peppercorns | — 8-10 |
| Salt | — to taste |

## *Method :*

1. Combine the egg white, cornflour, salt, chicken & leave to marinade for 15-20 mts.
2. Heat the vegetable oil in a heavy-bottomed pan & stir-fry the marinated chicken (along with the marinade) for about 1 mt.
3. Remove with a slotted spoon.
4. Add all other ings (except the seeds & spring onions) to the pan & bring the mixture to a boil.
5. Lastly, add the chicken & spring onions & cook for 1-2 mts.
6. Serve at once garnished with sesame seeds.

# 9. CHICKEN WITH CASHEWNUTS

## Serves—4

*Calories—208 per portion*

*Ingredients :*

|  |  |
| --- | --- |
| Boneless chicken breasts (skinned) | — 350 gms |
| Spring onions (chopped) | — 4 |
| Ginger (chopped finely) | — 1" |
| Garlic (chopped finely) | — 2-3 |
| Egg white | — 1 |
| Dry sherry | — 2 tbsps |
| Cornflour | — 2 tsps |
| Vegetable oil | — 2 tbsps |
| Soya sauce | — 1 tbsp |
| Cashewnuts | — 50 gms |
| Salt | — to taste |

## *Method :*

1. Cut the chicken into small cubes.
2. Combine the egg white, cornflour & half the sherry.
3. Add the chicken & toss well till well coated.
4. Heat the oil in a heavy-bottomed pan & stir-fry the onions garlic & ginger for a few seconds.
5. Add the chicken & stir well.
6. Pour in the other ings & cook till the chicken is tender. Serve at once.

# 10. CHICKEN PULAO

## Serves—4

*Calories—395 per portion*

***Ingredients :***

| | |
|---|---|
| Chicken portions | — 4 |
| Long-grain rice (cooked) | — 100 gms |
| Vegetable oil | — 2 tbsps |
| Chicken stock | — 150 ml |
| Dry cider | — 150 ml |
| Saffron (powdered) | — pinchful |
| Onion (chopped) | — 1 (large) |
| Garlic (minced) | — 3 cloves |
| Ginger (minced) | — 1" |
| Mushrooms (chopped) | — 100 gms |
| Chilli powder | — ½ tsp |
| Turmeric powder | — ¼ tsp |
| Garam masala powder | — ¼ tsp |
| Pepper | — to taste |
| Salt | — to taste |
| Coriander leaves (chopped) | — to garnish |

## *Method :*

1. Heat the oil in a heavy-bottomed pan & fry the chicken portions along with the onion, ginger garlic & mushrooms, till golden.
2. Add the rest of the ings (except the rice & saffron) one by one & cook covered for about 1 hour.
3. Stir the saffron into the cooked rice.
4. Arrange the rice on a serving dish, put the chicken pieces & vegetables on top & serve hot garnished, with coriander leaves.

# (F) MEAT

A DELIGHTFUL CHOICE OF RECIPES FROM MANY DIFFERENT COUNTRIES IS PROVIDED IN THIS CHAPTER. THERE ARE PLENTY OF WHOLESOME CASSEROLES FOR FEEDING THE FAMILY AS WELL AS MORE SOPHIS TICATED DISHES FOR SPECIAL OCCASIONS

# 1. DELICIOUS LAMB CHOPS

## Serves—4

*Calories—466 per portion*

*Ingredients :*

| | |
|---|---|
| Lamb chops (trimmed) | — 8 |
| Butter | — 15 gm |
| Onion (thinly sliced) | — 1 |
| Cooking apples (peeled, cored & sliced) | — 2 |
| Raisins | — 2 tbsp |
| Dry cider | — 150 ml |
| Pepper | — to taste |
| Salt | — to taste |

## *Method:*

1. In a non-stick pan, melt the butter, add onion & fry till soft. Remove & spread half of it over the bottom of a casserole.
2. Cover with half the apple slices, sprinkle half the raisins & seasoning.
3. Brown the chops in the pan till brown on both sides, drain & place in the casserole.
4. Cover with the leftover onion & apples & sprinkle with the remaining raisins, & seasoning. Pour in the cider.
5. Cover the casserole & cook in the oven for about 1½ hours or until the chops are tender. Serve hot.

***USEFUL TIP** : Enjoy this dish with a crisp green side salad.*

## 2. APRICOT STUFFED LAMB

### Serves—6

*Calories—431 per portion*

*Ingredients :*

| | |
|---|---|
| Shoulder of lamb (boned) | — 1 (1.5 kg) |
| Apricots (dried) | — 175 gms |
| Onion (chopped finely) | — 1 (big) |
| Mint leaves (chopped finely) | — 2 tsps |
| Breadcrumbs | — 75 gms |
| Egg (beaten) | — 1 |
| Pepper | — to taste |
| Salt | — to taste |

### *Method :*

1. Soak the apricots in water for 6-8 hr.
2. Drain & reserve the liquid. Chop the apricots & combine with the onion, mint leaves & breadcrumbs.
3. Add the egg & a little apricot soaking liquid (if required) to bind. Sprinkle the seasoning & mix well.
4. Spoon the stuffing into the lamp bone cavity & secure with a string.
5. Cook in the oven for about 2 hrs or until well cooked.
6. Serve hot by cutting into thick slices.

# 3. LAMB STUFFED WITH PALAK

## Serves—4

*Calories—174 per portion*

*Ingredients :*

| | |
|---|---|
| Knuckles end boned lamb leg (trimmed) | — 1 (400 gms) |
| Spinach (chopped, cooked & drained) | — 225 gms |
| Mint leaves (chopped finely) | — 15 gms |
| Garlic (chopped finely) | — 4-5 |
| Vinegar | — 1 tsp |
| Red wine | — 175 ml |
| Sugar | — pinchful |
| Salt | — to taste |
| Pepper | — to taste |
| Mint leaves | — to garnish |

## *Method :*

1. Mix together all ings (except lamp leg & red wine).
2. Lay the lamb leg flat with the boned side up & spread the spinach mixture over.
3. Fold the meat over & secure with a string.
4. Lay the leg in an oven proof roasting dish, pour the wine over, adding a little water if needed & cook in the oven for about an hr.
5. Cut into thick slices, pour off the excess fat & serve hot garnished with mint leaves.

# 4. PAPRIKA LAMB

## Serves—4

*Calories—233 per portion*

*Ingredients :*

| | |
|---|---|
| Mutton chops | — 4 |
| Onion (chopped finely) | — 1 |
| Natural low-fat yoghurt | — 150 ml |
| Paprika | — 2 tsps |
| Parsley sprigs | — to garnish |

***For the marinade :***

| | |
|---|---|
| White wine | — 2 tbsps |
| Lemon juice | — 2 tsps |
| Dried thyme | — ½ tsp |
| Sugar | — to taste |
| Pepper | — to taste |
| Salt | — to taste |

## *Method :*

1. Combine all the ings for the marinade & place the chops in the mixture for 4-6 hrs.
2. Drain, place in an oven proof dish, sprinkle onion on top, cover with a foil & cook the chops in a moderately hot oven for about 1 hr.
3. Mix together the yoghurt & the paprika & spoon over the chops.
4. Cook for another 15 mts & serve hot garnished with parsley.

# 5. ORANGE FLAVOURED MUTTON

## Serves—4

*Calories—316 per portion*

***Ingredients :***

| | |
|---|---|
| Mutton (cut into small cubes) | — 500 gms |
| Red chillies (seeded & chopped) | — 2 |
| Orange (cut into slices) | — to garnish |

***For the marinade :***

| | |
|---|---|
| Tomato puree | — 2 tbsps |
| Onion (grated) | — 1 (small) |
| Orange rind | — 1 tbsp |
| Orange juice | — 1 tbsp |
| Honey | — 2 tsps |
| Tabasco | — 2-3 drops |
| Red wine | — 2 tbsps |
| Paprika | — 1 tsp |
| Olive oil | — 2 tbps |

## *Method :*

1. Combine the mutton cubes with all the ings for the marinade, cover & keep in the fridge for 6-8 hrs.
2. Drain & reserve the marinade.
3. Arrange the mutton cubes on 4 skewers with the red chilli pieces.
4. Spoon the marinade over the cubes & cook in a moderately hot oven for half-an-hour or under a moderately hot grill for 15-20 mts turning once or twice.
5. Serve hot garnished with orange slices.

# 6. YUMMY MUTTON KEBABS

## Serves—4

*Calories—347 per portion*

*Ingredients :*

| | |
|---|---|
| Mutton (cut into small cubes) | — 450 gms |
| Orange rind (grated) | — 1 tsp |
| Onion (cut into thin slices) | — 1 (small) |
| White wine | — 150 ml |
| Peppercorns (coarsely crushed) | — ¼ tsp |
| Cinnamon (powdered) | — pinchful |
| Salt | — to taste |

*For the sauce :*

| | |
|---|---|
| Onion (chopped finely) | — 1 (small) |
| Artificial liquid sweetener | — to taste |
| Natural low-fat yoghurt | — 2 tbsps |
| Egg yolk | — 1 |
| Cornflour — 1 tsp | Olive oil — 1 tbsp |
| Orange juice — 1 tbsp | Saffron (powdered) — pinchful |

## *Method :*

1. Combine together the mutton cubes, wine, orange rind, onion slices, peppercorns, cinnamon, salt & leave to marinade (covered) for about 2½-3 hrs.
2. Drain the cubes, reserving the marinade & thread onto skewers. Grill for 4-5 mts or till well browned under moderate heat.
3. Heat the oil in a heavy-bottomed pan & fry the chopped onion for 2-3 mts.
4. Add the strained marinade & saffron. Bring to a boil.
5. In the meanwhile, blend the egg yolk with the orange juice, cornflour & yoghurt. Add to the sauce & let the sauce thicken a little, stirring continuously.
6. Add the sweetener.
7. Serve the grilled kebabs accompanied by the sauce.

# (G) DESSERTS

THE DESSERT COURSE, USUALLY VERY HIGH IN CALORIES, OFTEN PROVES TO BE AN IRRESISTABLE TEMPTATION TO WEIGHT-WATCHERS THE RECIPES INCLUDED HERE, SHOW HOW FAVOURITE DESSERTS INCLUDING ICE-CREAMS CAN STILL BE ENJOYED AS A PART OF LOW CALORIE DIET. FRUIT IS THE OBVIOUS CHOICE AS A BASE FOR LOW-CALORIE DESSERTS VISUALLY APPEALING & NATURALLY SWEET, IT CAN BE COMBINED WITH OTHER INGREDIENTS TO MAKE BOTH HOT & COLD DESSERTS. NATURAL LOW-FAT YOGHURT IS USED INSTEAD OF CREAM IN THESE RECIPES.

# 1. STUFFED FIGS

## Serves—4

*Calories—94 per portion*

*Ingredients :*

| | |
|---|---|
| Fresh ripe figs | — 12 |
| Almonds (ground) | — 3 tbsp |
| Fresh strawberries (chopped) | — 100 gms |
| Honey | — 1 tbsp |
| Lettuce leaves | — 4 |

## *Method :*

1. Snip off any excess stalk from each fig, make a criss-cross cut down from the stalk end & carefully ease the cut open.
2. Mix together the almonds with the strawberries & honey.
3. Place a lettuce leaf, spread out flat, on each serving plate,arrange three figs on top of each one & fill with the raspberry & almond puree.
4. Serve at once.

***USEFUL TIP :*** *The stalk end of a ripe fig should feel slightly soft when pressed. If it is still hard, leave to ripen at room temperature.*

# 2. FRESH FRUIT SALAD

## Serves—4

*Calories—83 per portion*

*Ingredients :*

|  | |  |
|---|---|---|
| Apple (sliced) | — | ½ |
| Pear (seeded & sliced) | — | ½ |
| Banana (peeled & sliced) | — | ½ |
| Pineapple (peeled, cored & chopped) | — | ½ |
| Black grapes (halved & seeded) | — | 50 gms |
| Strawberries (sliced) | — | 50 gms |
| Honey | — | 1 tbsp |
| Water | — | 60 ml |
| Lemon juice | — | ½ tbsp |
| Lemon rind (grated) | — | ½ tsp |
| Oranges (peeled, pith removed & segmented) | — | 1-2 |

## *Method :*

1. Bring to a boil the water along with the honey & lemon rind.
2. Simmer for2-3 mts & keep aside to cool after straining.
3. Stir in the lemon juice.
4. Pour the lemon syrup over the fruits, mix well & put to chill in the fridge.
5. Serve very chilled.

# 3. BAKED FRUIT SALAD

## Serves—4

*Calories—79 per portion*

***Ingredients :***

| | |
|---|---|
| Grape fruit (sliced with the peel) | — 1 |
| Oranges (sliced with the peel) | — 2 |
| Dry Apricots (cut into halves) | — 8 |
| Apple (sliced thinly) | — 1 |
| Fresh orange juice | — 300 ml |

## *Method :*

1. Mix together all fruits in an oven proof casserole.
2. Pour in the orange juice & cover with a foil.
3. Bake in the oven for about 15-20 mts, until all the fruit is soft.
4. Serve hot or cold as per choice.

# 4. APRICOT & BANANA DELIGHT

## Serves—4

*Calories—130 per portion*

***Ingredients :***

| | |
|---|---|
| Bananas (peeled & sliced) | — 2 |
| Dried apricots (soaked in water overnight) | — 100 gms |
| Raisins | — 25 gms |
| Lemon juice | — 2 tsps |
| Natural low-fat yoghurt | — 150 ml |
| Artificial liquid sweetener | — to taste |
| Nutmeg (grated) | — to taste |

### *Method :*

1. Sprinkle lemon juice on the sliced bananas.
2. Place the apricots in a bowl with a little of the soaking liquid. Add the bananas & raisins.
3. Divide this mixture into the parts.
4. Sweeten the yoghurt if you like so, spoon over the fruit & sprinkle with grated nutmeg.
5. Chill thoroughly & serve.

# 5. PEAR DELIGHT

## Serves—4

*Calories—83 per portion*

*Ingredients :*

| | |
|---|---|
| Firm pears (peeled) | — 4 |
| Fresh orange juice | — 250 ml |
| Red wine | — 120 ml |
| Cardamoms (powdered) | — ½ tsp |
| Artificial liquid sweetener | — to taste |

## *Method :*

1. Put the pears in an oven proof dish, pour the orange juice & wine, sprinkle cardamom powder & bake in the oven for 30-40 mts.
2. Taste for sweetness & serve either hot or chilled with the strained juices.

# 6. FRUIT WITH HONEY

**Serves—4**

*Calories—113 per portion*

*Ingredients :*

| | |
|---|---|
| Bananas (cut into thick slices) | — 2 |
| Pears (peeled, cored & chopped) | — 2 |
| Dried apricots (chopped) | — 8 |
| Apples (cored & cut into slices) | — 2 |
| Pineapple (peeled & chopped) | — 2 tbsps |
| Lemon juice | — 2 tsps |
| Dry cider | — 2 tbsps |
| Honey | — 2 tsps |
| Mint leaves (chopped finely) | — to garnish |

## *Method :*

1. Put the fruits in an oven proof dish.
2. Mix together the remaining ings & pour over the fruits.
3. Cover & cook in the oven for half an hour.
4. Garnish with mint leaves, chill for a few mts & serve.

# 7. FRUIT COCKTAIL

## Serves—4

*Calories—83 per portion*

*Ingredients :*

| | |
|---|---|
| Bananas (peeled & sliced) | — 2 |
| Peaches (peeled, stoned & sliced) | — 2 |
| Raisins | — 25 gms |
| Lemon juice | — 2 tsps |
| Fresh orange juice | — 4 tbsps |
| Raspberries (pureed) | — 150 gms |
| Nutmeg (grated) | — pinchful |

## Method :

1. Put the fruits in a bowl along with raisins.
2. Sprinkle with lemon juice. Add the orange juice & stir gently. Keep aside for about 30-45 mts.
3. Divide the fruit into four portions.
4. Spoon a portion of raspberry puree over each serving to decorate & sprinkle nutmeg.
5. Chill thoroughly & serve.

# 8. STRAWBERRY FREEZY WONDER

## Serves—6

*Calories—68 per portion*

### *Ingredients :*

| | |
|---|---|
| Strawberries (pureed) | — 250 gms |
| Cottage cheese (crumbled) | — 225 gms |
| Natural low-fat yoghurt | — 150 ml |
| Powdered gelatine | — 3 tsps |
| Egg whites (beaten till stiff) | — 2 |
| Water | — 3 tbsps |
| Artificial liquid sweetener | — to taste |
| Strawberries (halved) | — to garnish |

## *Method :*

1. Dissolve the gelatine in the water over a pan of boiling water. Keep aside to cool.
2. Mix together the strawberry puree, cottage cheese & yoghurt. Fold in the gelatine mixture.
3. Add sweetener to taste. Also fold in the egg whites.
4. Pour into a flat tin & chill for about 3 hours or until set.
5. Remove divide into 4 portions, garnish with halved strawberries & serve.

# 9. LEMON YOGHURT DELIGHT

## Serves—4

*Calories—174 per portion*

*Ingredients :*

| | |
|---|---|
| Lemon juice | — 2 tbsps |
| Lemon rind (grated) | — ½ tsp |
| Natural low-fat yoghurt | — 450 ml |
| Honey | — 1 tbsps |
| Dry sherry | — 2 tbsps |
| Fresh fruits (chopped) | — to garnish |

## *Method :*

1. Whisk the yoghurt with the honey & lemon rind.
2. Gradually add the lemon juice & sherry, stirring continuously.
3. Divide the mixture into four serving dishes or bowls & serve chilled.

# 10. STRAWBERRY ICE-CREAM

## Serves—4

*Calories—79 per portion*

*Ingredients :*

| | |
|---|---|
| Fresh ripe strawberries (hulled) | — 350 gms |
| Egg yolks | — 3 |
| Redcurrant jelly | — 1 tbsp |
| Red vermouth | — 1 tbsp |
| Natural low-fat yoghurt | — 300 ml |
| Strawberries (halved) | — to garnish |

## *Method :*

1. Blend together the egg yolks, jelly, vermouth, yoghurt & half the strawberries, until smooth.
2. Transfer the mixture into a shallow container, and freeze until the ice-cream starts to harden around the edges.
3. Beat the ice-cream to break up the ice-crystals.
4. Chop the remaining strawberries & mix into the ice-cream mixture.
5. Return to the container & freeze until firm.
6. Scoop the ice-cream into serving bowls & serve garnished with halved strawberries.

# 11. RASPBERRY ICE-CREAM

## Serves—4

*Calories—206 per portion*

***Ingredients :***

| | |
|---|---|
| Raspberries (liquidised) | — 225 gms |
| Natural low-fat yoghurt | — 900 ml |
| Icing sugar | — 50 gms |
| Honey | — 2 tbsps |
| Lemon juice | — 2 tbsps |
| Mint leaves | — to garnish |

## *Method :*

1. Mix together all ings along with the liquidised raspberries, stir thoroughly & freeze until well set.
2. Scoop the ice-cream into serving bowls & serve garnished with mint leaves.

***NOTE :*** *Set the refrigerator at its lowest temperature when freezing this icecream in order to get the best results.*

# 12. ORANGE SERVE-ME-SOON

## Serves—4

*Calories—179 per portion*

*Ingredients :*

| | |
|---|---|
| Fresh orange juice | — 3 tbsps |
| Lemon juice | — 3 tbsps |
| Curd cheese | — 350 gms |
| Powdered gelatine | — 4 tsps |
| Skimmed milk | — 3 tbsps |
| Artificial liquid sweetener | — to taste |
| Orange (cut into slices) | — to garnish |

## *Method :*

1. Dissolve the gelatine in the orange juice in a bowl over a pan of gently simmering water.
2. Blend in the remaining ings spoon into individual serving dishes or bowls & serve chilled garnished with orange slices.

# 13. ORANGE & PINEAPPLE JELLY

## Serves—4

*Calories—109 per portion*

*Ingredients :*

| | |
|---|---|
| Orange jelly crystals | — 1 packet |
| Fresh pineapple juice | — 200 ml |
| Water | — 150 ml |
| Natural low-fat yoghurt | — 150 ml |
| Orange (cut into thin slices) | — to garnish |

## *Method :*

1. Heat the water, add the jelly crystals & stir until completely dissolved stir in the pineapple juice.
2. Pour into a bowl & place in the fridge till it starts setting.
3. Whisk in the yoghurt,pour into 4 serving bowls & leave until set.
4. Garnish with orange slices & serve.

# 14. ORANGE-HONEY WONDER

## Serves—4

*Calories—65 per portion*

*Ingredients :*

| | |
|---|---|
| Orange juice | — ½ cup |
| Orange rind (grated) | — 2 tsps |
| Honey | — 25 gms |
| Lemon juice | — 2 tsps |
| Natural low-fat yoghurt | — 300 ml |
| Egg whites (beaten till stiff) | — 2 |

## *Method :*

1. Blend together the juices with honey.
2. Stir in the rind & yoghurt.
3. Fold the eggs into the mixture.
4. Spoon into four serving dishes, chill for a few mts & serve.

***NOTE :****Do not chill for more than 1 hour or else the mixture will start separating.*

# 15. BLACKCURRANT SURPRISE

## Serves—4

*Calories—54 per portion*

*Ingredients :*

| | |
|---|---|
| Skimmed milk | — 300 ml |
| Blackcurrants | — 300 gms |
| Cornflour (mixed with ½ cup milk) | — 1 tbsp |
| Artificial liquid sweetener | — to taste |
| Water | — 1 tbsp |
| Natural low-fat yoghurt | — 150 ml |
| Blackcurrants | — to garnish |

## Method :

1. Heat the milk, stir in the cornflour mixture and heat, stirring continuously until the mixture thickens. Add sweetener to taste and leave to cool.
2. Trim and wash the blackcurrants and put in a pan with the water. Cook over a low flame, until the fruit softens. Add sweetener to taste and let cool.
3. Puree the fruit in a blender.
4. Add the fruit puree and yoghurt to the milk mixture and whisk until very well blended.
5. Transfer into four individual serving dishes, decorate with blackcurrants and serve thoroughly chilled.

# 16. IRRESISTABLE COFFEE SORBET

## Serves—4

*Calories—99 per portion*

*Ingredients :*

| | |
|---|---|
| Natural low-fat yoghurt | — 600 ml |
| Skimmed milk powder | — 4 tbsps |
| Instant coffee powder | — 4 tbsps |
| Artificial liquid sweetener | — to taste |

*Method :*

Combine all the above ings, pour into a shallow dish & freeze for 2-3 hrs. The mixture should be served when quite soft.

# (H) DRINKS

WHEN ON A SLIMMING DIET, IT IS PARTICULARLY ESSENTIAL TO MAINTAIN A GOOD INTAKE OF FLUIDS & LONG, REFRESHING DRINKS CAN ALSO HELP TO WARD OFF HUNGER PANGS! A BLENDER. IS INVALUABLE IN CREATING VITAMIN-PACKED FRUIT & VEGETABLE COCKTAILS OR NUTRITIOUS DRINKS WHICH CAN BE DRUNK AT ANY TIME OF THE DAY OR NIGHT. HERE'S AN ARRAY OF SUCH DRINKS WHICH IS GOING TO BE A BOON TO SLIMMERS & HEALTH-CONSCIOUS

# 1. FRUIT WONDER

## Serves—4

*Calories—101 per portion*

*Ingredients :*

|  |  |
| --- | --- |
| Orange juice (fresh & unsweetened) | — 175 ml |
| Lemon juice (fresh & unsweetened) | — 175 ml |
| Pineapple juice (fresh & unsweetened) | — 175 ml |
| Grapefruit juice (fresh & unsweetened) | — 175 ml |
| Egg whites (beaten till stiff) | — 4 |
| Pepper | — to taste |
| Salt | — to taste |
| Soda water | — to top up |
| Mixed fruit (chopped) | — to garnish |

## Method :

1. Shake together all ings (except soda water) well & strain into a 1 litre jug.
2. Top up with soda water & pour into individual glasses to serve.
3. Spear thin pieces of fruit onto cocktail sticks to garnish. Serve at once.

***USEFUL TIP :*** *Always taste any food or drink after it has been chilled as chilling can quite remarkedly affect the amount of flavouring or sweetening required.*

# 2. STRAWBERRY DELIGHT

## Serves—4

*Calories—79 per portion*

*Ingredients :*

| | |
|---|---|
| Strawberries (hulled) | — 450 gms |
| Fresh orange juice | — 2 tbsps |
| Natural Low-fat yoghurt | — 450 ml |
| Gingerale (dry) | — 450 ml |
| Red food colour | — few drops |
| Ginger (ground to a paste) | — to taste |
| Strawberries (hulled) | — 4 (to garnish) |
| Crushed ice | — to taste |

## *Method :*

1. Blend together the strawberries, orange juice & yoghurt with some crushed ice until smooth.
2. Divide between 4 tall glasses.
3. Add the gingerale, food colour & stir.
4. Sprinkle ground ginger stir well & serve at once garnished with 1 strawberry per glass.

# 3. TEA PUNCH

## Serves—4

*Calories—94 per portion*

*Ingredients :*

| | |
|---|---|
| Hot tea (not very strong) | — 1 liter |
| Oranges | — 5 |
| Lemons | — 1 |
| Cinnamon | — ½" |
| Dark rum | — 60 ml |
| Artificial sweetener | — to taste |

## *Method :*

1. Peel a thin layer of skin from one of the oranges & steep it in the freshly made hot tea.
2. Squeeze the juice out of all fruit except one half orange & one half lemon.
3. Strain the juices & heat gently with the cinnamon.
4. Slice the half orange & half lemon as thinly as you can & soak the slices in rum.
5. Combine the heated juice with the tea, add the rum along with fruit slices. Stir in the sweetener.
6. Remove the cinnamon stick before serving.

# 4. WHOLESOME DRINK

## Serves—4

*Calories—266 per portion*

***Ingredients :***

| | |
|---|---|
| Porridge oats | — 75 gms |
| Apples (peeled,cored & chopped) | — 2 |
| Orange juice | — 1½ cups |
| Orange rind (grated) | — 1 tsp |
| Skimmed milk | — 300 ml |
| Butter milk | — 300 ml |
| Eggs | — 2 |
| Honey | — 2 tbsps |
| Cornflakes | — to garnish |

## *Method :*

1. Keep the porridge oats soaked in the skimmed milk overnight in the fridge.
2. Bring to a boil the orange juice along with the apple & orange rind.
3. Let simmer for few mts & then cool & let chill in the fridge overnight.
4. Blend together the porridge oats, skimmed milk along with all other ings mentioned till smooth.
5. Serve into 4 tall glasses garnished with cornflakes.

# 5. COOL DELIGHT

## Serves—4

*Calories—113 per portion*

*Ingredients :*

| | |
|---|---|
| Raspberries (crushed) | — 225 gms |
| Mineral water | — 300 ml |
| Water | — 1 tbsp |
| Dry white wine | — 275 ml |
| Fresh cream | — 1 tbsp |

## *Method :*

1. Bring to a boil the crushed strawberries along with water.
2. Simmer for another 2-3 mts. Keep aside to cool.
3. Combine the above mixture with all other ings mentioned, pour into an airtight container & refrigerate for 8-10 hrs.
4. Serve strained in tall glasses.

# 6. CHILLED TOMATO JUICE

## Serves—4

*Calories—26 per portion*

*Ingredients :*

| | |
|---|---|
| Ripe tomatoes (peeled & chopped) | — 500 gms |
| Tomato puree | — 1 tsp |
| Lemon juice | — 1 tsp |
| Brown sugar | — 1 tsp |
| Worcestershire sauce | — 1 tsp |
| Water | — 300 ml |
| Salt | — to taste |
| Lemon (cut into thin slices) | — to garnish |
| Mint leaves | — to garnish |
| Pepper | — to taste |

## *Method :*

1. Blend together all ings for about 1 mt.
2. Strain & chill for about 2 hrs.
3. Serve in tall glasses garnished with mint leaves & lemon slices.